# Our Family Roots From Nigeria Africa

The journey of the Ancestors of Jenny and Joe McLean From Igboland Nigeria Africa to Virginia then onto Cumberland and Harnett County North Carolina.

Written by Deena Porcaro Hill

2023

# Our Family Beginnings

## Journey from Igboland Nigeria to America

This is a very difficult story to tell and even harder to imagine, but I must tell it in honor of the great sacrifice made by our ancestors so many years ago.

## Igbo life

Our story begins in Ebem, Ohafia, Nigeria thousands of years ago. This region of Nigeria is part of what is now called Igboland. It is thought that the Igbo people inhabited the South East region of Nigeria where the town of Ebem, Ohafia is located along with the surrounding area for thousands of years. Igbo land is made up of five states which are, Anambra, Abia, Imo, Ebonyi, and Enugu.

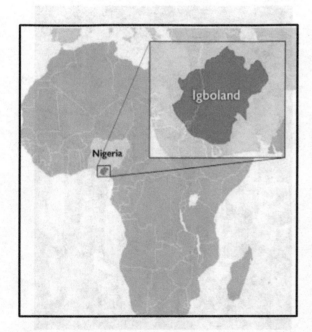 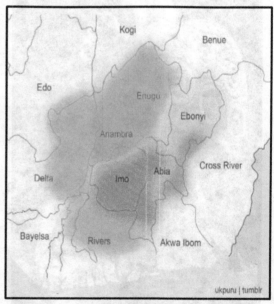

Our Ancestors were living in the state of Abia in the early 1700s. The Igbo people lived in small villages as farmers working just to eat and survive. They also enjoyed times of joy and happiness with family and friends eating foods such as yams, beans, and rice and dancing while enjoying Igbo traditions carried on from their ancestors.

During this time period, there were many wars and conflicts between neighboring villages. Warring villages would take prisoners and would take them to the town authorities. The Portuguese and the British began buying these captured slaves from Africa to be shipped around the world which started the global slave trade of the Igbo people and other African tribes.

## Our DNA connection to the Igbo

You may be wondering how we know we have a connection to the Igbo tribe of Nigeria. Well, thank goodness for the amazing science of DNA. To date of this writing, 20 descendants of Jenny and Joe McLean are a DNA match to members of the Igbo tribe; 12 of which are descendants of Nelson Holder Ritchie, my third great-grandfather. Each DNA match was born in Igboland Nigeria and come from families that have lived there for generations. Through DNA we have verified that we have Igbo blood. I have been in contact with almost all of our Nigerian-born Igbo DNA matches and they have been sharing with me their genealogy. Unfortunately, almost all of their genealogy is verbal, and much of it was lost with the Trans- Atlantic Slave Trade. Many of the people taken from their tribe were the ones who knew the family genealogy, making it very hard, if not impossible to trace ancestors very far back.

Donald Ritchie and Eni Njoku

**3rd cousin 1x removed** | Paternal side

< 1% shared DNA: 20 cM across 1 segments

We always hoped we could connect Jenny and Joe McLean to people in Africa, like Alex Haley author of the book "Roots" did. Through DNA it is happening to us. Conversely, it is interesting to talk with our family from Igboland Nigeria, and to hear them say how excited they are to find their descendants of those that were taken long ago. I had never thought of them looking for me. The realization of this connection is so precious to me.

## The Capture

Our 6th great-grandmother Jenny McLean's parents would have been a part of the many Igbo tribe members that were captured and taken to the Cave Temple Complex in Arochukwu Nigeria. Jenny's parents were probably captured while working in the fields and their children would have been at home caring for each other, then in an instant, all their lives were turned upside down forever.

From the moment of capture their nightmare began. Captured Igbo tribe members would be blindfolded and marched to the Cave Temple Complex tunnels of no return. The Cave Temple Complex was a center for ceremonial rites, knowledge, wisdom, and matters of tribal justice. Later on, it also became a place of enslaving tribal members and bargaining with the British and others.

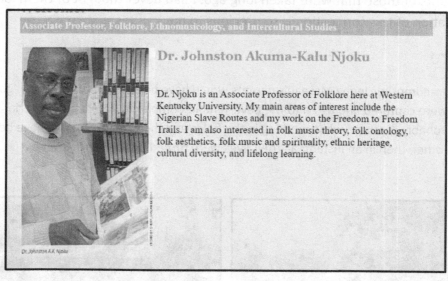

Associate Professor, Folklore, Ethnomusicology, and Intercultural Studies

### Dr. Johnston Akuma-Kalu Njoku

Dr. Njoku is an Associate Professor of Folklore here at Western Kentucky University. My main areas of interest include the Nigerian Slave Routes and my work on the Freedom to Freedom Trails. I am also interested in folk music theory, folk ontology, folk aesthetics, folk music and spirituality, ethnic heritage, cultural diversity, and lifelong learning.

Dr. Johnston A.K. Njoku

Professor Akuma Kalu Njoku[1] has studied the path of tears for many years and is a member of the Igbo tribe. He has personally walked this painful journey. Professor Akuma Kalu Njoku and his colleagues walked the very path that led to the entrance of the cave and traveled the long journey to the ports where the slave ships were docked. Professor Njoku has very generously allowed me permission to use his research to describe what our Grandparents would have endured in this process of enslavement. Below are excerpts from his research.

*"Thousands of Igbo victims of the Atlantic slave trade came from the hinterland, they were not declared slaves until they were ritually processed, symbolically declared dead and covertly funneled through cave tunnels that led to the coastal towns of Bonny, Calabar and Brass for the forced journey across the Atlantic Ocean. Most of those that traveled from Bonny went directly to Virginia."* This journey from capture to being loaded on a slave ship would have taken months, even before the journey began. The captured slaves were held for weeks in makeshift rock cells and sometimes chained to the roots of the very large Achi tree, along the journey to the ships and once on the ship would have been held for up to a month while enough slaves were captured to fill the ship.

Captives for sale were tied to this surface root of the achi tree

*The trail will lead to an ancient Cave Temple Complex in Arochukwu, Nigeria. In pre- Atlantic slavery times, the people of Arochukwu (the Aro) had performed customary rites for Chukwu (The Great Spirit) in the Cave Temple Complex. As the ritual specialists and custodians of the Temple, the Aro alone could enter the cave and into the Dark Chamber Presence of Chukwu, and through a major Oracle (Ibin Ukpabi) interpret the voice of Chukwu. At that time, the Ancient Cave Temple Complex was the highest court of justice in Igboland. People from all over Igboland went to the Temple to seek the truth from Chukwu Abiama (The Great Spirit to which Seekers of Truth Come) and to hear judgments through the Oracle. Those found guilty were either sold on to slavery or put to death depending upon the degree of their offence and the judgments of Chukwu. The blood of those that received the death penalty colored the running stream in the cave red. It was named the River of Blood. At the cave entrance from which the River of Blood flowed, families waited to receive news on the judgment and fate of the accused by the blood flowing in the stream or not.*

*It was with the advent of the Atlantic Slave Trade in the 17th century that the Aro, assuming the role of the leaders of the trade in the Igbo hinterland, exploited the Temple Complex in a very terrible way, by using it as a major secret slave dealing location. During this time the Aro took captured victims to the Temple Complex in what appeared to be the same ritual that had been undertaken since before memory, but as the victims disappeared into the cave tunnels (the tunnels of disappearance), the Aro would falsely color the river red with dye from the red cam wood to leave the impression that the condemned had died. The red water flowing from the cave was a signal to the relatives that the victims were dead. In reality, some of the tunnels led to various exist points on the trade routes to the coastal towns of Calabar and Bonny. One of the outlets led to Iyi Eke, a point from where the enslave, now blindfolded, were led to Onu Asu Bekee, or European Beach in Ito and from there to waiting boats took the slaves to Calabar for onward transmission to the New World of slavery. Another outlet led to Afia Oso Nwamkpi a slave market in Ututu from where, using He-Goat as a metaphor, Aro traders and escorts took victim to major hinterland slave markets in Bende, Uzuakoli and Azumini, before the Middle Passage."*

Road to the Arochukwu Temple Cave

The River of Blood

Cave entrance

Cave entrance

Professor Njoku was also quoted in an interview:

*"Professor Njoku and his colleagues also traveled through the Azumini to Arochukwu hinterland trail in Nigeria. It is a trail of pain. The idea of slave dealings in the Temple of God with direct links to Shipping Ports along the Slave Coast is painful. Entering the Chamber Presence and facing the exact place which the slave dealers took the victims of the Atlantic slave trade for judgment and ritual processing, to the exact place where thousands of African slaves entered and symbolically died is breathtaking. Following the tunnels of disappearance through the trade routes to the point where the Atlantic Oceans ends in a twilight zone is heartrending. The experience can be overwhelming and the story bitter, but it is the truth. It is the truth that must be told in order to begin to make real the reconnection with Africa, enhance reconciliation and forgiveness, and start the healing of the deep-seated wounds of the Atlantic slave trade and slavery on both sides of the Atlantic."*

The slave route to the Blue River showing the grove covering the gully

Ahia Afor, the busiest slave market in the 19th Century

The final stop at the slave quarters by the Blue River before traveling to Bonny

The Blue River

Nigerian relics of the slave trade from the 1600-1800

LEG IRONS ONCE USED ON ENSLAVED PEOPLE ON DISPLAY AT THE KURA HULANDA MUSEUM ON THE CARIBBEAN ISLAND OF CURAÇAO. CREDIT: AMILCAR ABREU / ALAMY STOCK PHOTO

Slit drums used to summon the slaves

# The long Voyage

To this point, those enslaved have spent weeks or months of unimaginable physical pain, heartache, sadness, deprivation, and being separated from their loved ones as they traveled toward the slave ships.

Now was the moment of no return. I cannot imagine the thoughts that must have been going through their minds as the ship full of fellow Igbo tribe members took off for the great unknown. A world they could not comprehend.

The conditions on the ship were brutal and unbearable. Chained together in a space where they were stacked one beside another and their personal space was barely tall enough to sit up in and with no room to roll over or stretch out. They had to sit and sleep in their own feces and vomit. The slaves would only be allowed up on deck once or twice during the 6-8 week journey because of the fear of a slave revolt. Those who became sick with disease or died were thrown overboard.

### Old Calabar

Old Calabar, located in the Bight of Biafra, Nigeria, was a major port of the slave trade. Records show that during the peak years of the slave trade-from the late seventeenth to the mid-eighteenth centuries-699 identified ships left Old Calabar loaded with 205,600 Africans. The port's traffic represented more than 28 percent of the Africans deported from the Bight of Biafra. But Bonny was the leading port, with 1,048 identified ships carrying 384,000 Africans.

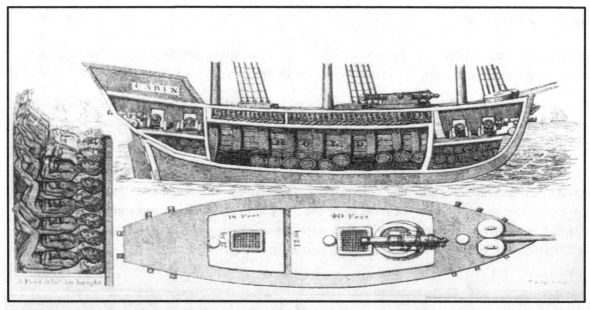

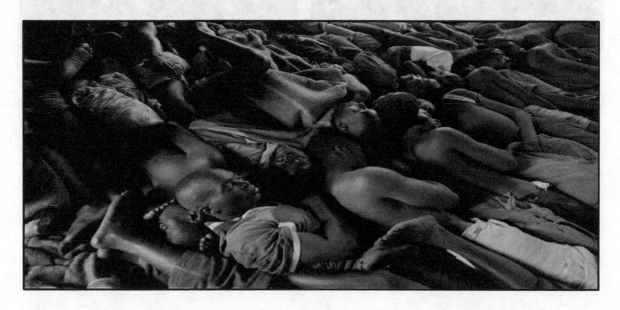

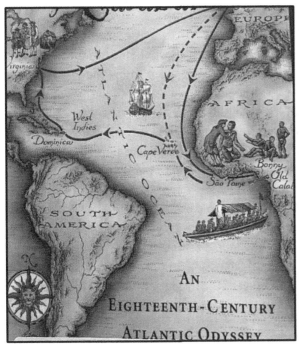

Bonny and Calabar to Virginia

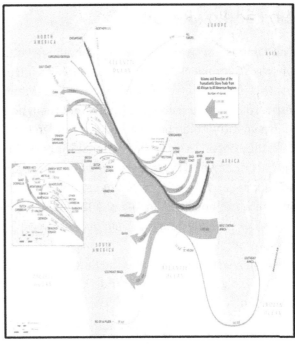

Red line - Bonny and Calabar to Virginia

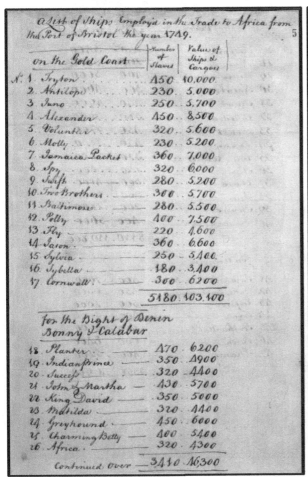

# Igbo Landing Revolt

One famous example was the Igbo Landing Revolt. It happened off the coast of St. Simons Island near Brunswick Georgia in 1803. The slave ship was full of Igbo slaves and was approaching the St. Simons port. The chained slaves were able to work together and overpower the ship's crew and threw the crew overboard. The ship then ran aground and the Igbo slaves chose to walk back into the water together and drown rather than be enslaved in a foreign land. As they walked into the water of nearby Dunbar Creek, they began to sing "The Water Spirit brought us, the Water Spirit will take us home". This was a major act of bravery. There were eyewitnesses to this event who were able to hand down the story of Igbo Landing and the events that happened there that day. There were a few slaves that were pulled from the water and lived. In Aug of 2023, my husband Gary, myself, my brother David, and his two girls Audrey and Clair, my nephew Tobin our cousin Desi, and some other cousins were able to attend the ceremony at Igbo Landing on St. Simons Island. The King of the Igbo, Eze Chukwuemeka Eri, attended along with several of his Chiefs. The King performed a memorial blessing on the waters and on the spirits of those who gave their lives for their freedom. This act of bravery is considered the first Freedom march in this country.

King Eze Chukwuemeka Eri        King offering a blessing upon Igbo landing

After the memorial blessing, we attended the annual Igbo Festival, in honor of the revolt at Igbo Landing, which included dancing, food, and ceremonial rites. During the festival we had the privilege to receive our Igbo name from the King, being descendants of the lost members of the Igbo tribe that were enslaved and sold in the Americas and other stops along the way. It was a life-changing event for us all. It was hard to imagine that we were actually reconnecting to our enslaved ancestors, those who were snatched from their homeland of Nigeria Africa, and were enslaved here in America in the 1700's.

King Eze Chukwuemeka Eri (center)

Audrey, Claire, and David Porcaro, Deena Porcaro Hill, Desi Campbell and Tobin Merrill receiving new Igbo name from King Eze Chukwuemeka Eri.

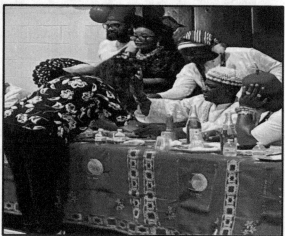

# Arriving in Virginia

My 7th great grandparents (parents of Jenny McLean) were from the Igbo tribe that arrived in Virginia around 1775. History has shown that the largest number of slaves shipped to the Richmond area of Virginia were from the Igbo tribe of Nigeria. On the 1880 Census of Harnett County North Carolina, our 6th great-grandmother Jenny McLean said that she was born in Virginia about 1785 and that her parents were both born in Africa.

| | | | | | | | | |
|---|---|---|---|---|---|---|---|---|
| | Margaret cw f 55 | Sister | | | | | | |
| | Mary A. w f 8 | Neice | | | | | | |
| 48 48 | McLean George B m 56 | | 1 | Farmer | | | | Virginia |
| | Venus B f 63 | wife | 1 | Keeping house | | | 31 | Virginia |
| | Jennie B f 95 | Mother | | | | Virginia Africa Africa | | |
| | Harrington Sophia B f 16 | Grnd daugh | 1 | | | N C N C N C | | |
| 49 49 | McDougald Albert B m 39 | | 1 | Farmer | | | | |
| | Rose B f 35 | wife | 1 | Keeping house | | | | |

Against all odds, Jenny's parents (my 7th great grandparents) survived the ocean voyage and all that they endured before that. Once in Virginia they were again held in chains and subjected to humiliation being placed on an auction block and prodded and examined and auctioned off to the highest bidder. We are not aware if Jenny's parents were able to remain together or if they were separated at the time, never to see each other again. We do know that Jenny was born in the Chesapeake Bay area of Virginia in about 1785, most likely, in Richmond. Jenny and her parents would have planted and picked tobacco in Virginia, tobacco being the main crop at the time.

What I imagine Jenny and her mother looked like

A slave auction

## Igbo Village-Staunton Virginia

In Staunton, Virginia an Igbo village has been built to replicate life in Nigeria and in remembrance of the Igbo slaves. Professor Akuma Kalu Njoku helped build the village. Below is an excerpt from Professor Njoku about the village.

*"The Igbo Village in Staunton, Virginia (also known as the 1700s West African Farm exhibit) is a tangible recognition of the contributions of Igbo victims of the Atlantic slave trade to development of Virginia and the greater American frontier culture. Enslave Igbo men, women and children who traveled by force from many specific locations in the hinterland of Igboland to North America, helped to build what is now known, as the United States.*

A great majority of those who came to Virginia boarded slave ships in the coastal towns of Calabar, Bonny and Brass. Evidently, one of the starting points of Igbo slave journeys is the ancient Cave Temple Complex in Arochukwu. Arochukwu traders supplied slaves to the market in Bende (later Uzuakoli) which became the source of slaves traveling directly from Bonny to Virginia.

An Igbo Farmstead will represent the architectural patterns representing the areas from, which most number of slaves came to Virginia. The Igbo were greater in number than all the other enslaved Africans put together in Virginia in the 1700s when tobacco was the mainstay of the colony's economy. Some estimates put the number of Igbo imported from the Bight of Biafra at 40% of all the imported to Virginia by 1775. Their number continued to increase to the point that tobacco planters on the valley west of the Blue Ridge replaced their white indentured servants with Igbo slave workers. The Igbo were among the first settlers. They were among those to cross the Cumberland Gap and open the gateway to the west.

In addition to making tobacco the mainstay of the Virginian economy, the Igbo also provided the labor in the Black Belt that made cotton king. They have continued to contribute to the nation building and culture in the United States. The Igbo Farmstead (Ulo Ubi Igbo) in Staunton is, like the English, German and Irish Farmsteads, a tangible tribute to the Igbo settlers who helped to develop the frontier culture in America as well as in the territorial expansion of the United States."

Ticha Akuma-Kalu Njoku (pictured) was a major contributor and volunteer in the construction of Igbo Village

## 1700s West African Farm

A large number of Africans (estimated at nearly 250,000) were brought to the Colonies from West Africa in the 1600s, 1700s and 1800s to work as servants, agricultural workers and artisans. They worked on farms, corn fields, cotton and tobacco plantations, with the highest concentration (approximately 40%) in Virginia and South Carolina. The first African slaves arrived in Virginia, for example, in 1619.

Due to this fact, the first farm on the grounds of the Museum is dedicated to reproducing a West African Village, specifically an Igbo household on the coast known as Bight of Biafra, nowadays located in Nigeria (since it is considered that many of the captives came from this area).

## The Coffle

When Jenny was about 8 years old she and her parents were again subjected to an unimaginable journey. In the 1700's there was a great need for slaves in the growing south, to plant and pick cotton and tobacco and make tar from the pitch of pine trees. There was a large growing market for slaves from Virginia. Slave traders in Virginia would round up a group of slaves, sometimes as many as one hundred. To transport the slaves they would shackle two men together by the wrist. They would also tie the wrists of two women together with rope. They would walk two by two in rows of up to 50. The slave traders would ride on horses with whips to ensure there would be no revolts and to make sure they kept up with the rest of the group. This was called a Coffle and it was a common site in Virginia and in many states south of Virginia. There were many eyewitness accounts of this atrocity recorded in journals. Sometimes the slaves had no shoes on their feet. Jenny and her parents were forced to walk in the extreme heat, 215 miles to Fayetteville North Carolina. Fayetteville was one of the stops along the way to the slave markets in Georgia, Alabama, and Mississippi. We believe Fayetteville is where the slave traders sold Jenny and her parents to John McNeill of Harnett County North Carolina and here they began life in another unknown place. How did they endure? It is beyond imagination.

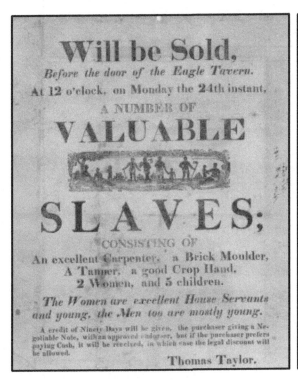

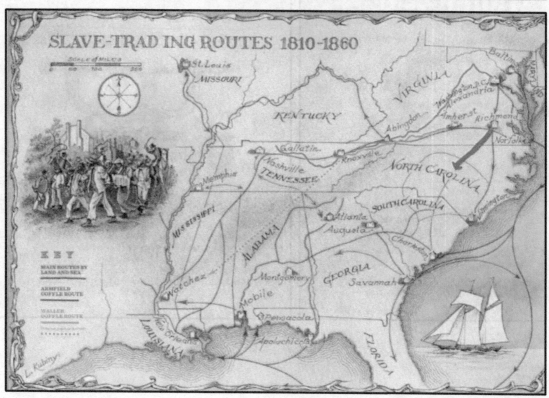

# Harnett County North Carolina

We do know that Jenny ended up being enslaved by John (Sober) McLean in 1793 in Cumberland (Harnett) County North Carolina. Jenny is listed in John (Sober) McLean's will, dated 1 Oct 1793.

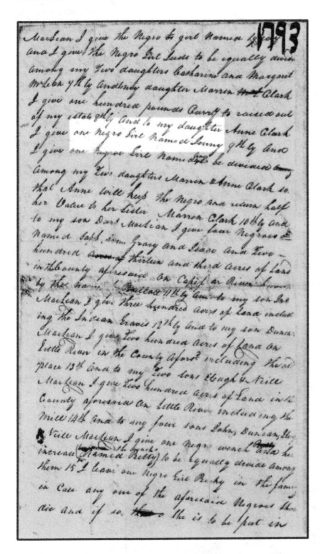

What I imagine Jenny McLean looked like

Jenny and her parents began their new life in Harnett County North Carolina planting and picking tobacco probably working 6 days a week from sun up to sun down in extreme heat and extreme cold. Many of the men worked in the making of turpentine used to seal the boats that came up the Cape Fear River. Jenny McLean met Joe McLean, who became my 6th great-grandparent and had at least 15 children that we can trace to our family through their descendant's DNA. There may be more that have not yet been connected through DNA. Jenny remained a slave her entire life. Jenny lived to be at least 95 years old, just imagine all that she had gone through. Jenny and Joe's children would remain slaves for a good portion of their lives in Harnett County and surrounding areas and surrounding states.

Hugh McC. Clark
to
Archibald McLean Jr.

State of North Carolina }
Cumberland County } Know all men by these presents
that I Hugh McC. Clark of the County and State aforesaid
for and in consideration of the sum of Two hundred & fifty Dollars to me in hand
paid by Archibald McLean Jr of the same County and State have granted bargained
_____

**a negroe Woman, named Jinny (the wife of Joe)** _____

bald McLean Jr his heirs Executors Administrators and assigns, against the lawful
claim or claims of myself my heirs, Executors administrators or assigns, and against
the lawful claim or claims of all and every other person or persons whomsoever.

In Witness whereof I have hereunto set my hand & affixed hereunto my
seal this second day of March A.D. 1838. ____

signed sealed & delivered }
in presence of }
Wm L McKay }

Hugh McClark (Seal)

State of North Carolina } Court of Pleas & Quarter Sessions
Cumberland County } March Term 1839. ―
Then was the Bill of Sale from Hugh McClark
to Archd McLean Jr proved in open court by the oath of Wm McL McKay and
ordered to be registered. ―――――

Test Jno. McLaurin Jr Clk

1838

Example of an enslaved family in North Carolina

Example of enslaved people planting tobacco

Tobacco crop in Harnett County North Carolina

Example of enslaved people making turpentine

A hard, sticky amber rosin, sometimes called pitch, was made from the trees' turpentine gum, or oleoresin. It was used to preserve ropes and rigging on sailing ships and to caulk the seams between timbers in the ships' hulls.

## Children of Jenny and Joe McLean:

2. **Sarah McNeill** born abt 1800 Cumberland County North Carolina she died after 1880 Harnett County, North Carolina. Married Sherod "Sherd" McNeill born abt 1797 North Carolina he died before 1880 Harnett County, North Carolina.

3. **Bett McNeill** born abt 1805 Cumberland County, North Carolina she died after 1880 Harnett County, North Carolina. Married _____ Smith born abt 1805.

4. **Celia McNeill** born abt 1806 Cumberland County, North Carolina she died after 1880 Wake County, North Carolina. Married Jack McLean born abt 1805 Cumberland County, North Carolina.

5. **Juda "Judie" McNeill** born abt 1807 Cumberland County, North Carolina she died after 1900 Lillington, Harnett, North Carolina Married Cyrus McLean born abt 1805 North Carolina.

6. **Tempy Jane McNeill** born abt 1808 Cumberland County, North Carolina she died abt 1888 Harnett County, North Carolina. Married Isaac Murchison born about 1808 Cumberland County, North Carolina he died 1895 Harnett County, North Carolina.

7. **Lilly "Lizzie" McNeill** born abt 1809 Cumberland County, North Carolina she died after 1870 Topeka, Shawnee, Kansas. Married _____ Richey.

8. **Milly McLean** born 12 July 1810 Cumberland County, North Carolina she died 14 Jan 1912 Harnett County, North Carolina. Married George McDougald born 12 June 1798 Cumberland County, North Carolina he died 22 Dec 1898 Cumberland County, North Carolina.

9. **John Robert "Bob" McNeill** born abt 1812 Cumberland County, North Carolina he died before 1900 Harnett County, North Carolina. Married Pheobe Williams Born Feb 1835 Cumberland County, North Carolina she died 17 Aug 1910 Harnett County, North Carolina.

10. **Lucy McLean** born abt 1815 Cumberland County, North Carolina she died after 1880 Newton County, Mississippi. Married Richard "Rich" Chapman born abt 1806 South Carolina he died after 1880 Newton County, Mississippi.

11. **Joseph "Joe" McLean** born abt 1816 Cumberland County, North Carolina he died before 1900 Harnett County, North Carolina. Married Rachael McCormick born 1 Jun 1833 Cumberland County, North Carolina she died 24 May 1926 Harnett County, North Carolina.

12. **George McLean** born abt 1818 Cumberland County, North Carolina he died after 1880 Upper Little River, Harnett, North Carolina. Married Venus Smith born abt 1814 Cumberland County, North Carolina she died after 1880 Upper Little River, Harnett, North Carolina.

13. **James "Jim" McLean** born abt 1819 Cumberland County, North Carolina he died after 1870 Barbecue, Cumberland, North Carolina. Married Hannah Bailey born abt 1843 Cumberland County, North Carolina she died after 1870 Barbecue, Cumberland, North Carolina.

14. **Sharper McNeill** born abt 1820 Cumberland County, North Carolina he died before Mar 1898 Cumberland County, North Carolina. Married Zylphia Ray born abt 1840 Cumberland County, North Carolina she died after 1880 Carvers Creek, Cumberland, North Carolina.

15. **Simon McLean** born abt 1816 Cumberland County, North Carolina. Married Mountain McDougald born about 1820.

Sarah McNeill was born in 1800 and is the oldest daughter of Jenny and Joe McLean. Different last names because a slave was made to take on the slave owner's last name. Sarah and Sherod McNeill are my 5th great-grandparents. Sarah and Sherod McNeill went on to have 14 children that we can tie our DNA to date. Sarah and Sherod McNeill had a daughter Jane McNeill born about 1820. Jane was sold to William Holder, where her name became Jane McNeill Holder, taking on the name of the slave owner.

Fayetteville North Carolina Slave Market

The Children of Sarah and Sherod "Sherd" McNeill:

1 **Elizabeth "Lizzy" "Bet" McNeill** born abt 1815 Cumberland County North Carolina she died 1909 Barbecue, Harnett, North Carolina. Married Daniel J. Harrington born abt 1835 Cumberland County North Carolina he died before 1880 Moore County, North Carolina.

2 **Mr. McNeill** born abt 1816 Cumberland County North Carolina he died after 1857 Harnett County, North Carolina. Married Maria ____ born abt 1816 Cumberland County North Carolina she died 23 June 1914 McNeill's Ferry Plantation, Harnett, North Carolina.

3 **Dianah McNeill** born abt 1817 Cumberland County, North Carolina she died after 1920 Maxton, Robeson, North Carolina. Married Henry B. McLean born abt 1815 Cumberland County, North Carolina.

4 **William "Billy" McNeill** born abt 1818 Cumberland County, North Carolina he died before 1880 Harnett County, North Carolina. Married Ammie born abt 1815 Cumberland County, North Carolina she died after 1880 Harnett County, North Carolina.

5 **Jane McNeill (Holder)** born abt 1820 Cumberland County, North Carolina she died 1843 Turnback, Lawrence, Missouri. Not Married but had a child with her white plantation owner Wiley Holder born 25 April 1812 Duplin County, North Carolina he died 2 June 1888 Harnett County, North Carolina.

6 **Stephen McNeill** born abt 1823 Cumberland County, North Carolina he died after 1871 Stewarts Creek, Harnett, North Carolina. Married Charlotte McNeill born abt 1838 Harnett County, North Carolina he died after 1871 Stewarts Creek, Harnett, North Carolina.

7 **Daniel C. McNeill** born Oct 1824 Cumberland County, North Carolina he died after 1880 Hoke County, North Carolina. Married Nancy McPhalter born 15 June 1825 North Carolina she died 1899 Hoke County, North Carolina.

8 **Gabriel McNeill (Bachus)** born abt 1825 Cumberland County North Carolina he died after 1900 Pensacola, Escambia, Florida. Married first wife, Caroline McLean born March 1827 Cumberland County, North Carolina she died after 1870 Harnett County, North Carolina. Married second wife, Maria born July 1852 Alabama.

9 **Charles McNeill** born abt 1826 Cumberland County North Carolina he died before 1900 Harnett County, North Carolina. Married Jennie McKoy born 1838 Cumberland County, North Carolina she died 25 Dec 1917 Upper Little River, Harnett, North Carolina

10 **Lettie McNeill** born abt 1827 Cumberland County North Carolina she died after 1900 Anderson Creek, Harnett, North Carolina. Married John McLean born abt 1820 Cumberland County, North Carolina.

11 **Hannah McNeill** born 1832 Cumberland County, North Carolina she died after 1867 Buckhorn, Harnett, North Carolina. Married Isaac Coffield born abt 1817 North Carolina.

12 **Dolly McNeill** born June 1835 Cumberland County North Carolina she died 8 Aug 1918 Arkansas. Married Reverand John Nelson born May 1829 Alexandria, Virginia he died after 1900 Owen, Pulaski, Arkansas.

13 **Sophie McNeill** born abt 1840 Cumberland County, North Carolina she died after 1880 Sand Hills, Moore, North Carolina. Married Americus Austin born abt 1822 North Carolina he died 8 Aug 1928 Addor, Moore, North Carolina.

14 **Cherry McNeill** born abt 1836 Cumberland County, North Carolina she died after 1880 Edgecombe County, North Carolina. Married Abraham Armstrong born abt 1816 Edgecombe County, North Carolina he died 22 June 1925 Wilson County, North Carolina.

An old neighbor of William Holder, a man by the name of Neal McNeill, made a trip from his home in Turnback, Lawrence, Missouri to visit his sister Flora C McNeill. Flora was a neighbor of William Holder. At that time William Holder had 5 slaves. Two of the slaves were Jane McNeill Holder and her two-year-old daughter Caroline. Caroline's father is unknown at this time but is most likely a slave of William Holder. Neal McNeill bought the 5 slaves from William Holder during his visit and took them back to Turnback, Lawrence, Missouri. In addition, Jane would have been almost 9 months pregnant at the time she was taken to Missouri. The father was William Holder's nephew, a white man named Wiley Holder. We know this because of the many DNA descendants of Wiley Holder that our family members match. This is one of those horrific instances you hear about of a white slave owner abusing and taking advantage of one of their slaves.

Example of pregnant enslaved girl      Picture of Jane drawn by descendant Bonnie Snyder

Jane McNeill Holder, taking the slave owner's last name, traveled almost 1000 miles back to Neal McNeill's home, being young and pregnant and scared. Who knows if she had to walk the whole 1000 miles or if she was lucky enough to ride in a horse-drawn wagon? Jane was ripped away from her family and the only place she ever knew in Harnett County North Carolina. Jane would never again see her family again. Jane died shortly after arriving in Missouri and after giving birth to my 3rd great grandfather, Nelson Holder Ritchie born 24 Aug 1840 in Turnback, Lawrence, Missouri.

Nelson Holder Ritchie

Nelson never knew his mother Jane because she died shortly after giving birth to Nelson. Jane probably died from having to make the 1000-mile journey being almost 9 months pregnant. The only family Nelson ever mentioned to his children was an old Scottish woman by the name of Nancy McNeill and his sister Caroline. Nancy McNeill was the mother of Neal McNeill who had bought the five slaves from William Holder, which included Jane. Nancy McNeill was probably the only person who ever showed love to Nelson and his sister Caroline. Nelson and Caroline would have lived on the McNeill farm and were about the same ages as McNeill's children.

Nancy McNeill, the woman who raised Nelson          Neal McNeill's children

Nelson told his children that people used to tell him he looked like his grandfather "Old Vincent". Nelson's father was Wiley Holder (a white man) and his father was George Vincent Holder, his nickname was "Old Vincent". George Vincent Holder had a son named George Vincent Jr, his nickname was "Young Vincent".

Nelson looks like his half-brother John Vincent Holder, from his white father's side

Nelson told his children his mother had dark skin. That is all Nelson told his children about his heritage, except when he was born, on 24 Aug 1840 in Lawrence County Missouri, and that his parents were born in North Carolina.

Nelson looks like his first cousin Sherd McNeill, from his black mother's side

The first we see Nelson on an official document of any kind is the listing of the slaves of Neal McNeill (the guy who bought the five slaves) on the 1850 Slave Census of Lawrence County Missouri. He is listed as a Mulatto (mix of black and white) and is 10 years old. His sister Caroline is listed as black (because she had a different father) and she is 12 years old. Caroline's father is probably one of the male slaves owned by William Holder (who sold the five slaves). Nelson and his sister were enslaved and would have worked long hours farming the McNeill land.

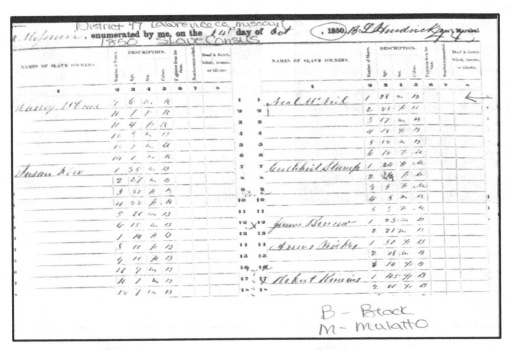

Neal McNeill's land in Turnback, Lawrence, Missouri where Nelson was born and where Jane died.

Neal McNeill land and cemetery. It is called McNeill Chapel Cemetery, there used to be a church on this property called the McNeill Chapel. Neal McNeill, slave holder of Jane, Caroline and Nelson is buried here.

Nelson ran away at the age of 15, possibly with his sister, and headed across the border to Kansas, which was a free state at the time.

Caroline the sister of Nelson, ended up in Wichita Kansas, married a man by the name of James Richey, and had one daughter named Anna Richey who married Abraham McAfee. Later, Caroline married a man named John Ratler. Caroline died when she was just 35 years old and is buried next to her daughter, without a headstone, in the Highland Cemetery in Wichita Kansas.

Highland Cemetery in Wichita Kansas

Mr. Nelson H. Richey came down last Friday from Great Bend, to attend the funeral of his sister, Mrs. Ratliff. Mr. Richey runs a first class livery and sale stable in Great Bend and a line of omnibuses connected with the railroad. He is an intelligent, enterprising and trustworthy colored man, and is a worthy example

Caroline Richey Ratler or Ratliff died July 1878 just 35 years old

We know that Nelson met up with Colonel John Ritchie an abolitionist operating the Underground Railroad in Topeka, Kansas. Colonel John Ritchie took Nelson into his home and Nelson took on the name of Ritchie.

Col. John Ritchie front row second from left. With a group of John Brown supporters.

Col. John Ritchie's home in Topeka Kansas-Historic Site of the Underground Railroad.
Nelson was listed in the Topeka City directory as living in this home in 1868.

Next time we see Nelson he is listed on the 1863 Civil War draft. He is listed as being 22 years old and colored. Nelson served in the Civil War in Oct 1864 for the Union Army in the 2nd Kansas State Militia. He served in the Calvary and was at the Battle of The Blue at Mockbee Farm. He told his children that he was shot at several times, but never wounded.

Nelson was in the 2nd Kansas State Militia Calvary at the Battle of the Blue.

Map of the battlefield

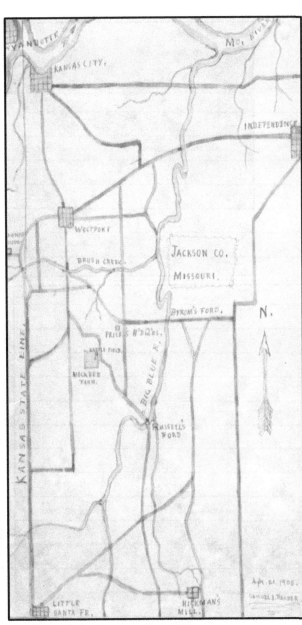

Nelson worked in Colonel Ritchie's limestone quarry as a teamster transporting the large blocks of limestone for the building of the Topeka Court House and the Lincoln College, later renamed Washburn University.

Col. John Ritchie's limestone quarry

Lincoln College Topeka Kansas

Plaque were Lincoln College stood and

Topeka Court House is in the background

Nelson's first wife was Mary Samantha Fulbright, a young Mulatto (mix of black and white) girl. They were married in 1870. Marys's mother's name was Minerva Fulbright, who was inslaved by William Fulbright. Mary's father was William Fulbright, the slave owner of Minerva.

William Fulbright lived in Springfield, Missouri for a time and then he moved to Topeka, Kansas, taking with him to Topeka, Kansas his enslaved girl Mary Fulbright who became the wife of Nelson Holder Ritchie.

In 1871 a baby boy named John Eddie Ritchie was born to Nelson and Mary. Both Mom and Baby died in 1871 and are believed to be buried in the Ritchie Cemetery in Topeka Kansas.

After the death of his first wife Mary and their new baby boy, Nelson along with his second cousin Josephus Richey, (Josephus changed the spelling to Richey), moved to Great Bend Kansas where they began a job as buffalo hunters. At the time the plains were overrun with buffalo giving them a good living.

Nelson and his second cousin Josephus Richey

Buffalo hunters in Great Bend, Kansas

In 1876 Nelson once again found love and married a beautiful young white woman by the name of Annie Cowan Russell, 17 years his younger. Nelson met Annie in St. John Kansas, she was working as a cook. They began their lives together in Great Bend managing several businesses they owned.

Annie Cowan Russell Ritchie

They owned the Union Hotel, livery stable, hack and dray wagons, horse-drawn omnibus, and mule-drawn cable cars. They were doing so well that they expanded their business to St. John Kansas and there, owned a second livery stable, and had plans to build a second hotel. Things were wonderful for a time and then many trials began to plague them. Their hotel burned, but they were able to rebuild it. Twice his livery stable blew down because of tornados and they had to rebuild those too. Nelson also faced discrimination being black in a predominantly white town and was the object of unkindness and prejudice.

Nelson's Livery Stable. Notice the N.H. Ritchie on the building. Nelson is standing on the left.

Hack and Dray wagons. Nelson worked picking up passengers and supplies from the Rail Road Station in Great Bend.

Nelson owned an Omni Bus and a Trolly Car picking up passengers from the train station.

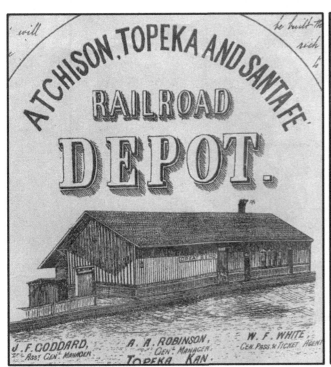

This is what the tain depot looked like when Nelson lived in Great Bend. What it looks like now in 2023.

While living in Great Bend 8 children were born to Nelson and Annie, two of the children died at a young age. Willie was 6 years old and died from complications of a broken hip that was caused by a fall off the front porch. Bertie was just over a year old and died of Typhoid fever. Nelson and Annie were broken-hearted but carried on the best they could for their remaining children.

Nelson Holder Ritchie and Annie Cowan Russell Ritchie's children

William (Willie) Ritchie

Bertie Elwood Ritchie

Olive Ellen Ritchie

James Alvie Ritchie

Elizabeth (Bessie) Ritchie

Annie May Ritchie

Blanche Ritchie

Esther Ritchie

Nelson Holder Ritchie Jr.

Grace Samantha Ritchie

Russell Dewey Ritchie

Elsie Virginia Ritchie

Willie Holder Ritchie

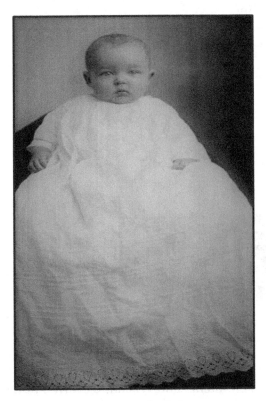

Bertie Elwood Ritchie

Nelson and Annie hired a man to help run their many businesses. This man soon after caused their financial ruin. Down and broke they decided to move to Bountiful Utah where Annie had lived as a child.

Bountiful Utah

Nelson's daughter's home in Bountiful, Utah. Olive Ellen Ritchie and William Cleverly's home where Nelson and Annie visited and stayed often. The home is still standing in 2023.

## William Henry Cleverly and Olive Ellen Ritchie Cleverly Family

Nelson's daughter Olive Ellen Ritchie, (my 2nd great grandmother) married William Henry Cleverly and had twelve children, (which included two sets of twins). Their daughter Louisa (Mary Louisa) Cleverly Day is my great grandmother. Mary Louisa had my grandmother Lillian Day Stonebraker. Lillian had my mother Jean Stonebraker Porcaro.

In 1861 Annie Cowan Russell, at the age of 4, and her family traveled 2000 miles from Pennsylvania to Salt Lake City Utah with the Mormon Pioneers. In Pennsylvania they had joined the Church of Jesus Christ of Latter-day Saints or at the time known as the Mormon religion.

Mormon Pioneer Wagon Train

While living in Utah 4 more children were born to them. Great sadness again struck when they lost their 2 ½-year-old son, Nelson Holder Ritchie Jr. to pneumonia. They also lost their 26-year-old daughter Annie May in childbirth while delivering her first child. They lost their 29-year-old daughter Blanche, who was pregnant with her 5th child, to pneumonia, and they also lost their 44-year-old son James Alvie to cancer of the jaw. Sadness and loss were a very large part of Nelson and Annie's life.

Nelson Holder Ritchie Jr.

Annie May Ritchie

Blanche Ritchie

James Alvie Ritchie

Nelson was now getting along in age and was not able to work as hard as he used to. He worked as a freight agent for the Union Pacific Railroad in Centerville, Utah until he injured his back.

He then bought a spring wagon and began selling fruit from the wagon and also tried his hand at raising turkeys and pigs. Just before going to market with the turkeys and pigs, someone had stolen them, which again was a huge financial loss.

Example of Turkey and Pig farmers

Annie and Nelson remained faithful members of the Church of Jesus Christ of Latter-day Saints until their dying days.

Nelson Holder Ritchie died 28 Jan 1913 in Salt Lake City Utah and is buried in the Bountiful Cemetery. Annie lived another 37 years alone without her dear husband, dying on 22 Mar 1950 and buried alongside her beloved husband in the Bountiful Cemetery.

Annie Cowan Russell Ritchie

Bountiful Utah Cemetary

# Summary

I marvel and am in awe that I am even here today when I look at the journey of my ancestors before me. How can I even begin to pay tribute or honor for their strength, courage, and fortitude to live each day as they did and to carry on their legacy? I feel very humbled and privileged to write of their journey, their heartache, their pain, and their triumphs. I know they are free from the pains and injustice of this world, and that makes me very happy. The wish of my heart is that someday I will be able to meet them and embrace them.

Footnote:

1. Dr. Johnston Akuma-Kalu Njoku. Associate Professor, Folklore, Ethnomusicology, and Intercultural Studies with ongoing fieldwork in Nigeria on the Trans-Atlantic Slave Trade in Africa.

Edited by my husband- Gary B. Hill

# Jenny or Jennie McLean

BIRTH  ABT. 1785 • Virginia, USA
DEATH  AFT. 1880 • Upper Little River, Harnett, North Carolina, USA
6th great-grandmother

## Facts

**Age 0 – Birth**
Abt. 1785 • Virginia, USA

**Age 85 – Residence**
1870 • Barbecue, Harnett, North Carolina, USA
Residence Post Office: Swains Station

**Age 95 – Residence**
1880 • Upper Little River, Harnett, North Carolina, USA
Marital Status: Widowed; Relation to Head: Mother

**Age 95 – Death**
Aft. 1880 • Upper Little River, Harnett, North Carolina, USA

**Jenny Parents born in Africa**
Africa

**Mother of Sarah McNeill**
Upper Little River, Harnett, North Carolina, USA
Desi Campbell and Deena Hill have determined that Jenny is the
Mother of Sarah McNeill because of DNA matches and the year
of her birth and that she was born in Virginia as Sarah McNeill
said her Mother was.

**George McLean and James McLean**
Harnett County, North Carolina, USA
We believe that George and James McLean are brothers of
Sarah. Jenny is living with son James or Jim in 1870 in
Barbecue,Harnett and with George in 1880 Upper Little
River,Harnett.Ages for Jenny Jennie are very different in both
census.But still her.

**Place of Birth**
Sarah said in the 1880 Census that her Mother was born in
Virginia

**Probate**
Cumberland, North Carolina, USA

## Family

### Parents

**Unknown Father Eni (IGBO)**
1750–

**Unknown Mother (IGBO)**
1755–

### Spouse and children

**Joe McLean**
1775–1852

**Sarah McNeill**
1800–1880

**Celia McNeill**
1803–1880

**Bett McNeill**
1805–1880

**Juda McNeill**
1807–1900

**Tempy Jane McNeill**
1808–1888

**Lilly or Lizzie McNeill (Ritchie)**
1809–1870

**Millie McLean**
1810–1912

**John Robert (Bob) McNeill**
1812–1900

**Lucy McLean**
1815–1880

**Simon McLean**
1816–

**Joseph Joe McLean**
1816–1900

**George McLean**
1818–1880

**James Jim McLean**
1819–1870

**Sharper McNeill**
1820–1898

## Sources

### Ancestry sources

1870 United States Federal Census

1880 United States Federal Census

North Carolina, Wills and Probate
Records, 1665-1998

# Unknown Father Eni (IGBO)

**BIRTH** ABT. 1750 • Ebem, Ohafia, Nigeria,Africa
**DEATH** Ebem, Ohafia, Nigeria,Africa

7th great-grandfather

## Facts

**Age 0 — Birth**
Abt. 1750 • Ebem, Ohafia, Nigeria,Africa

**Age 130 — Jennie's Parents**
1880 Census Jenny list both parents as born in Africa

**Death**
Ebem, Ohafia, Nigeria,Africa

## Family

Parents

Spouse and children

 **Unknown Mother (IGBO)**
1755-

 **Unknown Son 1 Eni (IGBO)**
1780-

 **Jenny or Jennie McLean**
1785-1880

 **Jude or Juda McLean**
1787-1870

# Joe McLean

**BIRTH** ABT. 1775 • Virginia
**DEATH** AFT. 1852 • Harnett County, North Carolina, USA
6th great-grandfather

## Facts

**Age 0 – Birth**
Abt. 1775 • Virginia

**Age 77 – Death**
Aft. 1852 • Harnett County, North Carolina, USA

**Place of Birth**
Sarah said in the 1880 Census that her Father was born in North Carolina.

**Probate**
Cumberland, North Carolina, USA

## Family

Parents

 Unknown Son 2 Elukpo (IGBO)
1750-

 Unknown Mother McLean (IGBO)
1755-

Spouse and children

 Jenny or Jennie McLean
1785-1880

 Sarah McNeill
1800-1880

 Celia McNeill
1803-1880

 Bett McNeill
1805-1880

 Juda McNeill
1807-1900

 Tempy Jane McNeill
1808-1888

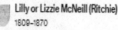 Lilly or Lizzie McNeill (Ritchie)
1809-1870

 Millie McLean
1810-1912

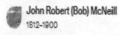 John Robert (Bob) McNeill
1812-1900

 Lucy McLean
1815-1880

 Simon McLean
1816-

 Joseph Joe McLean
1816-1900

 George McLean
1818-1880

 James Jim McLean
1819-1870

 Sharper McNeill
1820-1898

## Sources

Ancestry sources

 Geneanet Community Trees Index

 North Carolina, U.S., Wills and Probate Records, 1665-1998

 North Carolina, U.S., Wills and Probate Records, 1665-1998

# Unknown Son 2 Elukpo (IGBO)

BIRTH  ABT 1750 • Ihitenansa, Imo, Nigeria, Africa
DEATH  Ihitenansa, Imo, Nigeria, Africa

7th great-grandfather

## Facts

Age 0 – Birth
Abt 1750 • Ihitenansa, Imo, Nigeria, Africa

Death
Ihitenansa, Imo, Nigeria, Africa

## Family

Parents

 Unknown Father Elukpo (IGBO)
1730-

 Unknown Mother (IGBO)
1730-

Spouse and children

 Unknown Mother McLean (IGBO)
1755-

 Grace McLean
1773-

 Joe McLean
1775-1852

 Dorothy McLean
1776-1870

 Caden McLean
1780-1881

 Jim McLean
1782-

 Jack McLean
1796-1822

 Jacob McLean
1799-1822

# Sarah McNeill

BIRTH 1800 • Cumberland County, North Carolina, USA
DEATH AFTER 1880 • Harnett County, North Carolina, USA
5th great-grandmother

## Facts

Age 0 – Birth
1800 • Cumberland County, North Carolina, USA

Age 12 – Probate
10 Feb 1812 • Cumberland, North Carolina, USA

Age 41 – Probate
1841 • Cumberland, North Carolina, USA

Age 50 – Residence
1850 • Northern Division, Cumberland, North Carolina

Age 70 – Residence
1870 • Cross Creek, Cumberland, North Carolina, USA
Residence Post Office: Fayetteville

Age 80 – Residence
1880 • Upper Little River, Harnett, North Carolina, USA
Marital status: Widowed; Relation to Head of House: Mother

Age 80 – Death
After 1880 • Harnett County, North Carolina, USA

Residence
Harnett, North Carolina

## Family

Parents

 Joe McLean
1775–1852

Jenny or Jennie McLean
1785–1880

Spouse and children

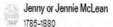 Sherod or Sherd McNeill
1797–1870

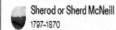 Elizabeth (Lizzy) McNeill
1815–1909

Dianah McNeill
1816–1920

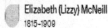 Mr McNeill
1817–1857

William ( Billy) McNeill
1818–1880

 Jane McNeill (Holder)
1820–1840

 Stephen McNeill
1823–1880

Gabriel McNeill (Bachus)
1825–1890

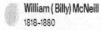 Charles McNeill
1826–1900

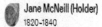 Lettie McNeill
1827–1900

Hannah McNeill
1832–1867

Wash McNeill
1833–

Dolly McNeill
1835–1918

Cherry McNeill
1836–1880

Sophie McNeill
1840–1880

## Sources

Ancestry sources

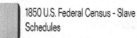 1850 U.S. Federal Census - Slave Schedules

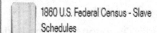 1860 U.S. Federal Census - Slave Schedules

 1870 United States Federal Census

 1880 United States Federal Census

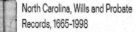 North Carolina, Wills and Probate Records, 1665-1998

 North Carolina, Wills and Probate Records, 1665-1998

Other sources

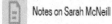 Notes on Sarah McNeill

# Sherod or Sherd McNeill

**BIRTH** ABT. 1797 • Cumberland County, North Carolina
**DEATH** BEF. 1870 • Harnett County, North Carolina, USA

5th great-grandfather

## Facts

Age 0 – **Birth**
Abt. 1797 • Cumberland County, North Carolina

Age 73 – **Death**
Bef. 1870 • Harnett County, North Carolina, USA

## Family

Parents

Father McNeill
1765-

Spouse and children

 Sarah McNeill
1800-1880

 Elizabeth (Lizzy) McNeill
1815-1909

Dianah McNeill
1816-1920

 Mr McNeill
1817-1857

 William ( Billy) McNeill
1818-1880

 Jane McNeill (Holder)
1820-1840

 Stephen McNeill
1823-1880

 Gabriel McNeill (Bachus)
1825-1890

 Charles McNeill
1826-1900

 Lettie McNeill
1827-1900

 Hannah McNeill
1832-1867

 Wash McNeill
1833-

 Dolly McNeill
1835-1918

 Cherry McNeill
1836-1880

 Sophie McNeill
1840-1880

# Father McNeill

**BIRTH** ABT. 1765
**DEATH** Unknown
6th great-grandfather

## Facts

Age 0 — **Birth**
Abt. 1765

## Family

Parents

Spouse and children

  **Samuel McNeill**
1785–1870

  **Backus McNeill**
1794–

  **Sherod or Sherd McNeill**
1797–1870

# About the Author
## My IGBO Heritage

Written by Deena Porcaro Hill    10 July 2023

Growing up as a child, I had a strong interest in our family's genealogy. One line on our family tree always held particular interest to me; it was my 3rd great-grandfather, Nelson Holder Ritchie's line, through my mothers side. The results of the research would miraculously change me and my family forever.

Living in Utah, I had access to the Salt Lake City Family History Library, one of the world's largest genealogical family history libraries. Years of research yielded little on the Ritchie line. In 2017 I decided to turn to DNA and take an Ancestry DNA test to help solve the mystery. I was unfamiliar with DNA, so I called Ancestry for assistance. They advised me to have the oldest living members of my family and the Ritchie family take the DNA test. I asked my 94-year-old Grandmother, her 93-year-old sister, and my mother, and of course, I would take the test also. In addition, I found, through my research, a wonderful gentleman named Don Ritchie, who I discovered later was, my cousin and the grandson of my 3rd great-grandfather, Nelson Holder Ritchie, who I have been looking for.

When the results came back, it showed that all four of us had African American DNA from Nigeria and the Ivory Coast of Africa. We were all shocked because we are white. There was no family lore of African heritage. Everything I knew about myself just changed. I was excited to know more.

One of the DNA matches was Desi Campbell of Harnett County, North Carolina. I reached out to him through Ancestry, and we began to write back and forth, exchanging family information. Early on during those exchanges, Desi asked if I knew that he was black. I wrote back and told him that I was white. The exchanges and research suddenly became daily phone conversations and an urgent quest.

Soon we found that Desi Campbell's 4th great grandfather and my 4th great grandmother were brother and sister and were both enslaved in Harnett County, North Carolina. We were ecstatic to establish our common ancestors. Because of this, we pushed forward to build the family trees that connected us and many other DNA matches. After seven years and thousands of hours of research and using DNA, Desi and I were able to build a family tree despite the lack of records of those that were enslaved.

What we found was that our 5th great-grandparents are Joe and Jenny McLean, who were enslaved in Cumberland (Harnett) County, North Carolina, and our 4th great-grandparents are Sarah (their daughter) and Sherd McNeill. Both sets of great-grandparents had 14 children each, and with the help of DNA, we have been able to identify and reunite with the descendants of each of these grandparents.

Jenny McLean (above) is the earliest ancestor we have found to date. She was born abt 1785 in Virginia, as stated in the 1880 Harnett County, North Carolina census. In the 1880 census, Jenny said that both her parents were born in Africa. This was an amazing and rare discovery to find a record of an enslaved person, Jenny McLean stating that her parents were born in Africa.

In June of this year (2023), Desi Campbell hosted an unprecedented DNA Reunion in Harnett County, North Carolina. Over 150 people were there to meet and connect with the McLean and McNeill family and their descendants. The reunion was amazing—discovery, tears, dance, and much explanation of how they were all connected, as you can imagine.

During this same time period, Desi and I discovered that members of our family showed five Nigerian-born DNA matches that are now US citizens. This would mean that the five Nigerians were matching because they were related to Jenny and Joe Mclean. Jenny and Joe were from the IGBO tribe.

Two of the five DNA matches are Eni Njoku and Oliver Udemba, both from Nigeria and both from the IGBO tribe. They have told us that only oral histories of their families were kept, and because of the slave trade, many of the names have been lost over the years. As I first mentioned, my cousin Don Ritchie shows as a 3rd cousin once removed to Eni, so that would mean they share the same 3rd or 4th great-grandparents. Because of the lack of records building an accurate family tree would be impossible. Instead, we have temporarily put Unknown IGBO born in Ebem, Ohafia, Nigeria, and Ihitenausa, Imo, Nigeria, in place of their actual names.

While getting to know Eni and Oliver, they told us that our ancestors stayed in the same villages for hundreds of years. With this information, we can place the origination of the parents of Jenny and Joe McLean to Ebem, Ohafia, Nigeria, and Ihitenausa, Imo, Nigeria. The link to Africa is now established.

A little backstory about Nelson Holder Ritchie: Nelson was enslaved in Lawrence County, Missouri, and ran away at the age of 15 to Kansas, which was a free state. Nelson was taken in by an abolitionist by the name of Colonel John Ritchie. From whom Nelson took on the name of Ritchie.

Nelson's mother, Jane McNeill Holder, was enslaved in Harnett County, North Carolina, and sold to a man in Lawrence County, Missouri. Nelson's mother, Jane died shortly after giving birth to Nelson. Jane had been enslaved in Harnett County, North Carolina, by a man by the name of William Holder. Jane had become impregnated by Wiley Holder, a nephew of William Holder. We know this because of the many DNA matches to the descendants of the Wiley Holder family.

Jane's mother and father, Sarah and Sherd McNeill, were enslaved by the McNeill family and their descendants in Harnett County, North Carolina. Sarah's parents were Jenny and Joe McLean, and they were enslaved by the McLean family and their descendants in Harnett County, North Carolina. Jenny's parents are unnamed at this time. We know they were born in Nigeria and belonged to the IGBO tribe. They were captured and sold in Ebem, Ohafia, Nigeria, and shipped to America, landing in Virginia. Their daughter Jenny, the 5th great-grandmother of Desi and I, was sold in Virginia and taken to Harnett County, North Carolina, sometime around 1793. We also see Jenny on the 1793 will of a white plantation owner Archibald McLean, in Harnett County, North Carolina.

This has been a life-changing journey for me. A white woman from Utah, and Desi Campbell, a black man from Harnett County, North Carolina, discovering our ancestry and family beginnings in Africa. I have been able to visit my black cousins in North Carolina, attending two McLean-McNeill family reunions and a third time to speak at the first African American Heritage Festival, organized by Desi Campbell. Desi has been able to visit Utah three times, once for a Ritchie Family Reunion (the white side of the family) and twice to attend RootsTech and stay in our home.

## Oliver Udemba family line-(DNA match)

Unknown Father Elukpo born abt 1730 Ihitenansa, Imo Nigeria Africa (Igbo Tribe)

Unknown Son Elukpo #1born abt 1745 Ihitenansa, Imo Nigeria Africa (Igbo Tribe)

Unknown Son Elukpo #2 born abt 1770 Ihitenansa, Imo Nigeria Africa (Igbo Tribe)

Unknown Son Elukpo #3 born abt 1800 Ihitenansa, Imo Nigeria Africa (Igbo Tribe)

Elukpo born abt 1830 Ihitenansa, Imo Nigeria Africa (Igbo Tribe)

Elesiobi born abt 1860 Ihitenansa, Imo Nigeria Africa (Igbo tribe)

Udamba Elesiobi born abt 1890 Ihitenansa, Imo Nigeria Africa (Igbo Tribe)

Okeke Fidelis Udemba born abt 1920 Ihitenansa, Imo Nigeria Africa (Igbo Tribe)

Oliver Udemba born abt 1950 Ihitenansa, Imo Nigeria Africa (Igbo Tribe)

## Nelson Holder Ritchie family line

Unknown Father Elukpo born abt 1730 Ihitenansa, Imo Nigeria Africa (Igbo Tribe)

Unknown Son Elukpo #2 born abt 1750 Ihitenansa, Imo Nigeria Africa (Igbo Tribe)

Joe McLean born abt 1775 born Virginia USA

Sarah McNeill born abt 1800 Cumberland County, North Carolina

Jane McNeill born abt 1820 Cumberland County, North Carolina

Nelson Holder Ritchie born 24 Aug 1840 Turnback, Lawrence, Missouri

## Eni Njoku family line-(DNA match)

Unknown Father Eni born abt 1750 Ebem, Ohafia, Nigeria Africa (Igbo Tribe)

Unknown Son Eni #1 born abt 1780 Ebem, Ohafia, Nigeria Africa (Igbo Tribe)

Unknown Son Eni #2 born abt 1820 Ebem, Ohafia, Nigeria Africa (Igbo Tribe)

Nna Eni born abt 1850 Ebem, Ohafia Nigeria Africa (Igbo Tribe)

Nna Njoku Eni born abt 1880 Ebem, Ohafia Nigeria Africa (Igbo Tribe)

Eni Njoku born 1917 Eben, Ohafia Nigeria Africa (Igbo Tribe)

Eni Gerald Njoku born 1950 Ibadan, Oyo Nigeria Africa (Igbo Tribe)


## Nelson Holder Ritchie Family Line

Unknown Father Eni born abt 1750 Ebem, Ohafia, Nigeria Africa (Igbo Tribe)

Jenny McLean born abt 1785 Virginia United States

Sarah McNeill born abt 1800 Cumberland County, North Carolina

Jane McNeill Holder born abt 1820 Cumberland County, North Carolina

Nelson Holder Ritchie born 24 Aug 1840 Turnback, Lawrence, Missouri

Russell Dewey Ritchie born 21 Nov 1898 Salt Lake City, Utah

Donald James Ritchie born 17 Mar 1938 Los Angeles, California

Record your family line.

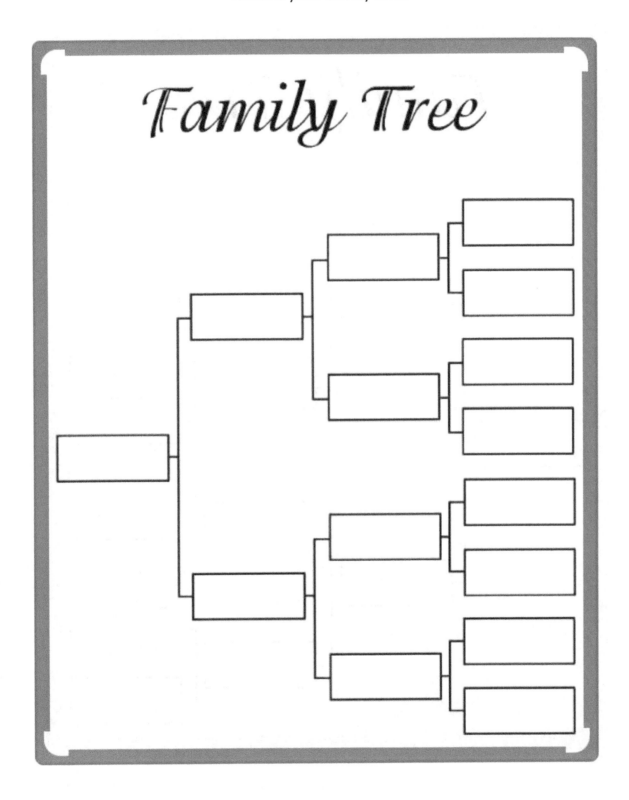

# Family Tree

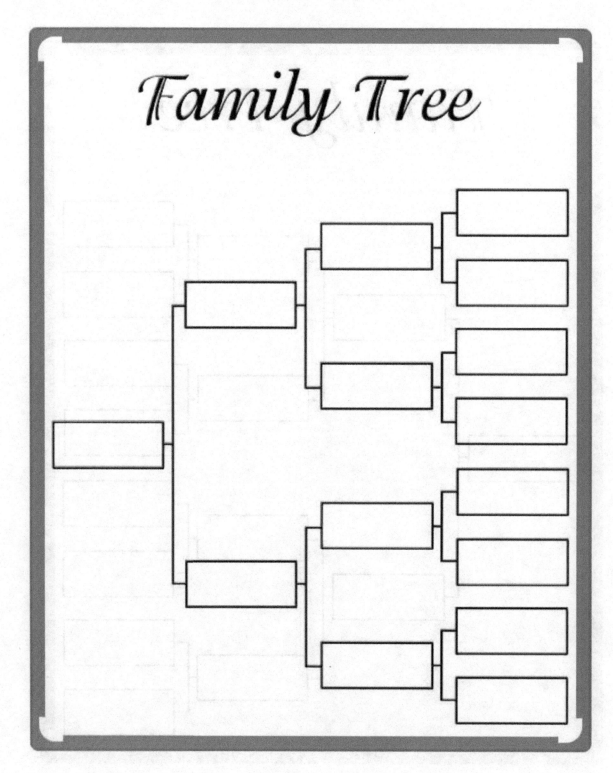

# Family Tree

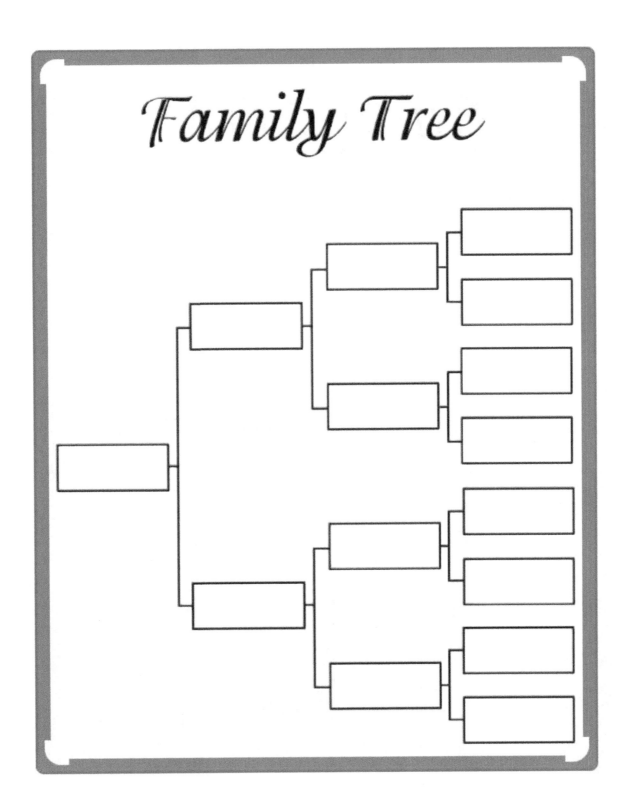

# Family Tree

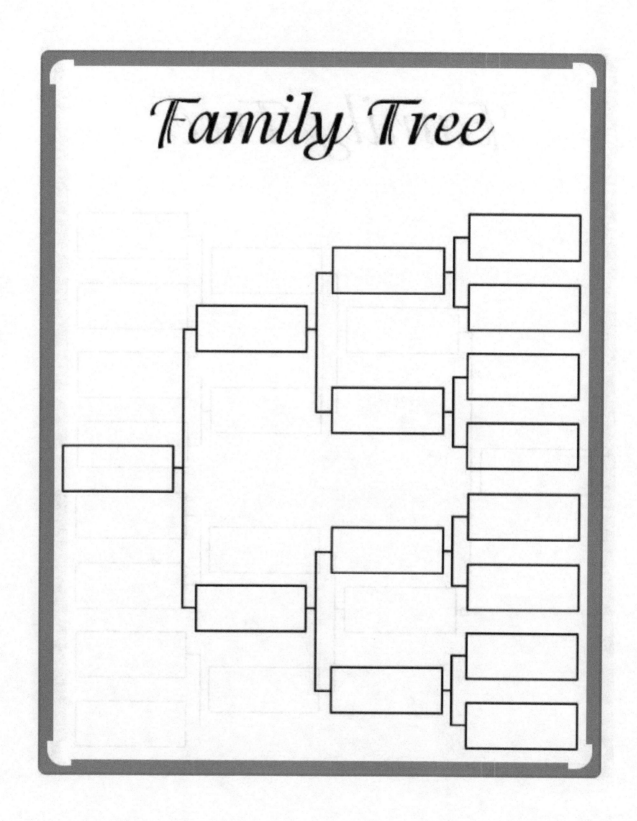

# Family Tree

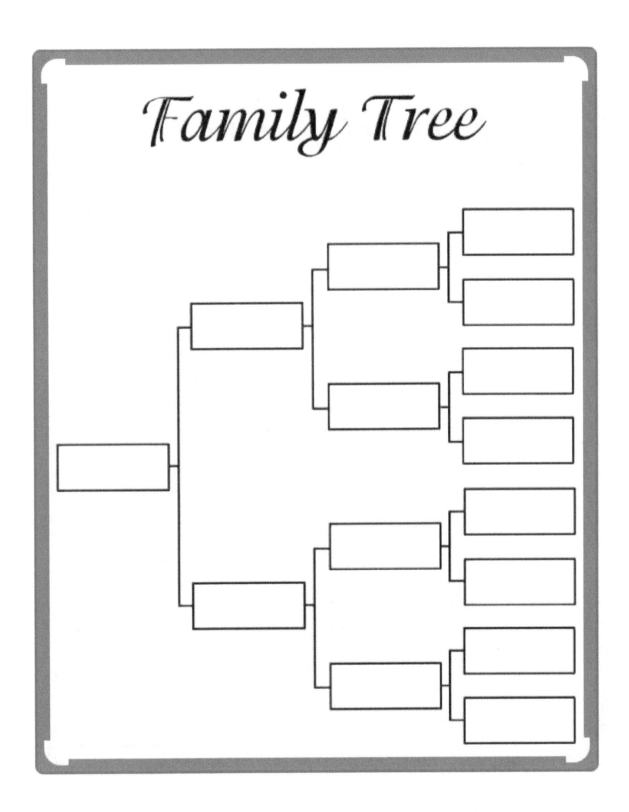

# Family Tree

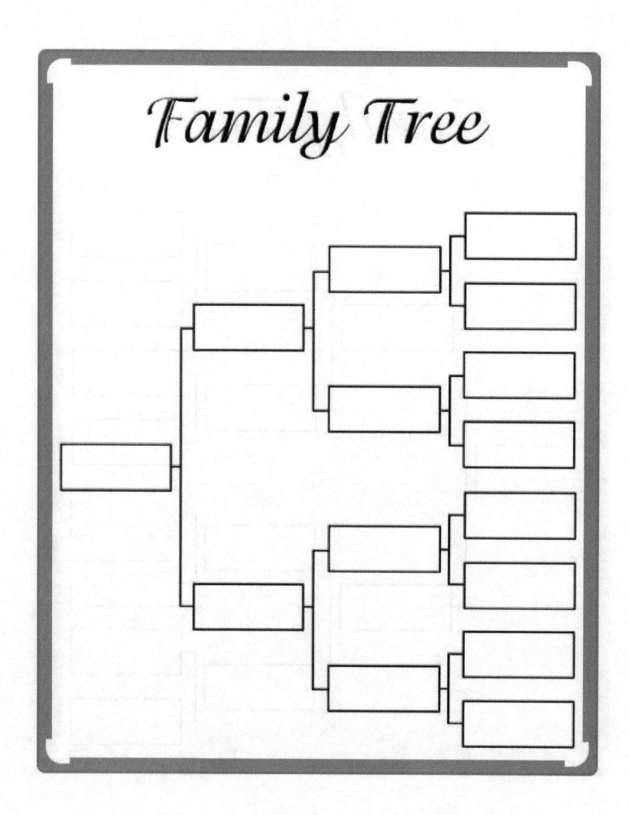

# Five Generation Family Tree

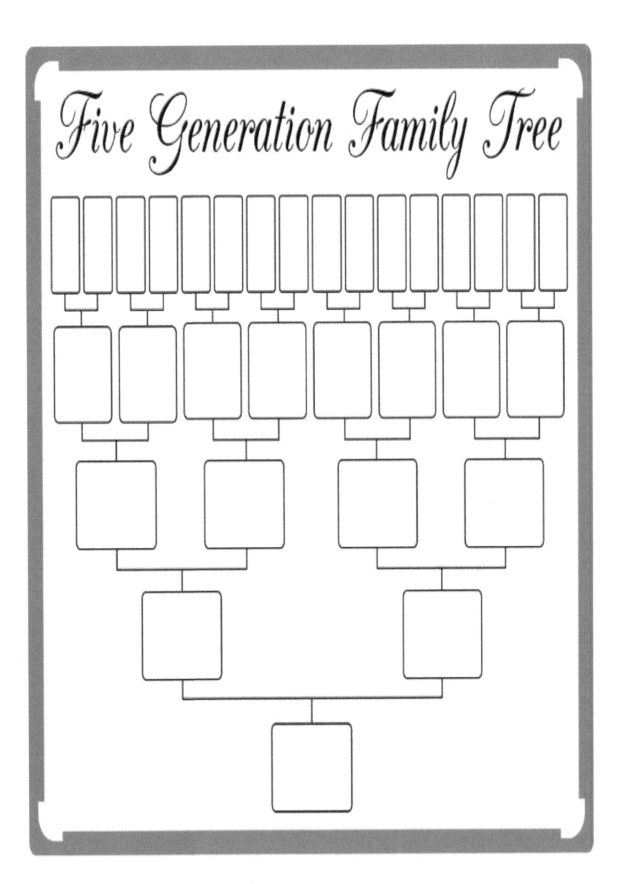

# Five Generation Family Tree

# Five Generation Family Tree

# Five Generation Family Tree

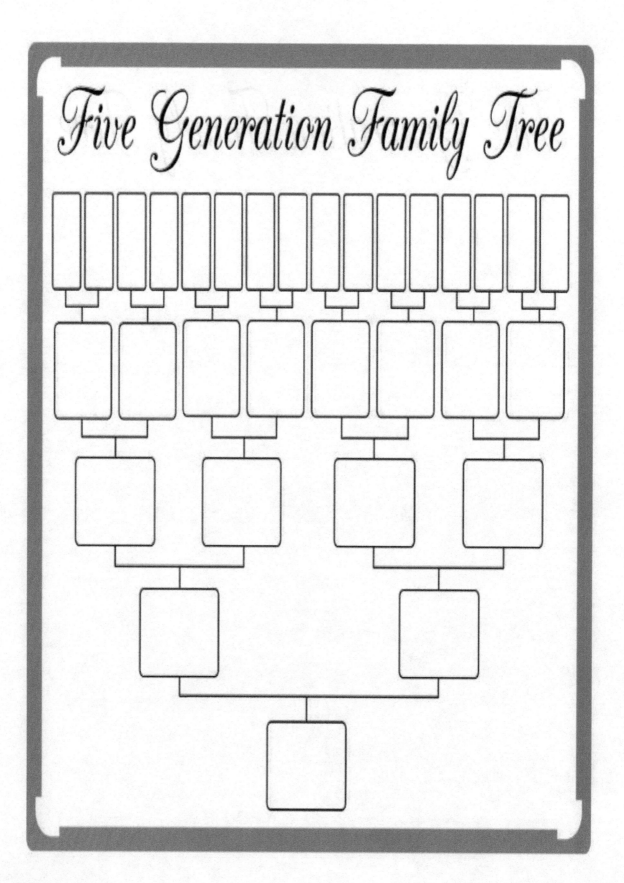

# Five Generation Family Tree

# Five Generation Family Tree

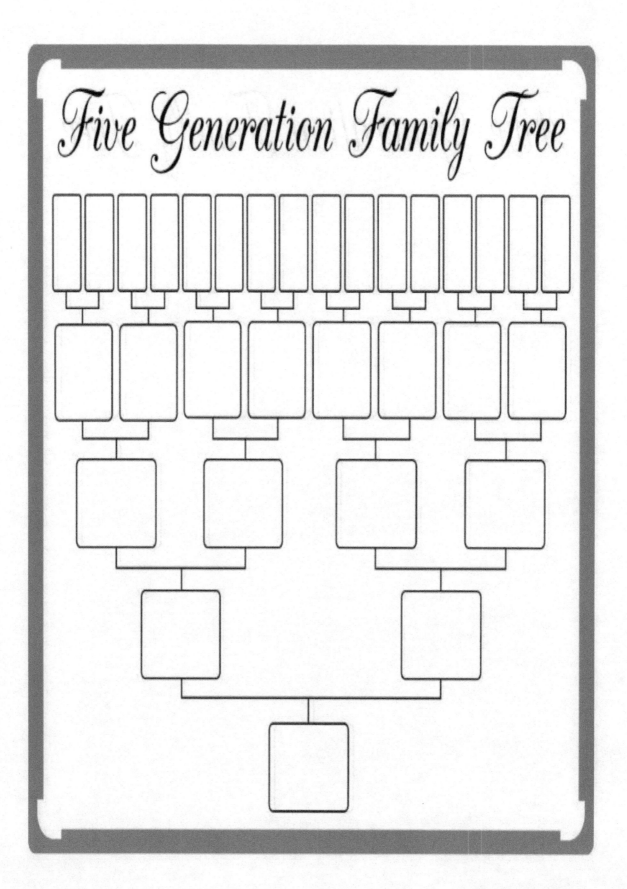

Made in the USA
Monee, IL
13 February 2024

53416466R20046